A true story from the Bible

Jesus and his friends were very busy helping everyone,

and they were tired!

But who's that?

People! More and more …

But Jesus cared about the people.

"Where can we get them some dinner?" he asked Philip. (Jesus knew really!)

"Dinner? For all these people?" said Philip.

"Loads and loads of money could only buy enough for a teeny, tiny bite each!"

"This boy has a sandwich to share,"
Andrew said,

"but it's only two little fish and five pieces of bread. That's not enough!"

and more, until more than five thousand people all had enough ... and there were leftovers!

How did Jesus do that with just one sandwich!?

Everyone was amazed, and they all wanted Jesus to be King!

But Jesus said, "You're just thinking about getting your dinner, which is all finished now."

"Didn't you see the amazing things I've been doing? They show you that God sent me …

they can have life that lasts **for ever,** not just for now!"

Notes for grown-ups

This story comes from John 6 v 5-15 and 25-35. Jesus and his disciples had found a quiet place to rest. In another account of this story, Mark tells us that they had been so busy helping people that they hadn't even had time to eat (Mark 6 v 31)! Even though Jesus needed a break, he felt sorry for the people who came looking for him. With one boy's five small loaves of bread and two fish, Jesus fed over 5,000 people.

Jesus' miracles were signs that show us who he is. But the people were not thinking about *who* could have such power, and did not see what they needed his help with most. They were just thinking about their food and how Jesus could make their lives better now. He told them, *"You are looking for me, not because you saw the signs I performed but because you ate the loaves and had your fill. Do not work for food that spoils, but for food that endures to eternal life"* (John 6 v 26-27, NIV).

Jesus told the crowd that he had come to give them something *much, much* better: *"Whoever comes to me will never go hungry, and whoever believes in me will never be thirsty"* (v 35, NIV). He went on to tell them that he would give his life to pay for our sins, so that anyone who believes in him will have life for ever, in heaven with God.

John 6 v 5-35
(The Bible: New International Version)

[5] When Jesus looked up and saw a great crowd coming towards him, he said to Philip, "Where shall we buy bread for these people to eat?" [6] He asked this only to test him, for he already had in mind what he was going to do. [7] Philip answered him, "It would take more than half a year's wages to buy enough bread for each one to have a bite!" [8] Another of his disciples, Andrew, Simon Peter's brother, spoke up, [9] "Here is a boy with five small barley loaves and two small fish, but how far will they go among so many?"

[10] Jesus said, "Make the people sit down." There was plenty of grass in that place, and they sat down (about five thousand men were there). [11] Jesus then took the loaves, gave thanks, and distributed to those who were seated as much as they wanted. He did the same with the fish. [12] When they had all had enough to eat, he said to his disciples, "Gather the pieces that are left over. Let nothing be wasted." [13] So they gathered them and filled twelve baskets with the pieces of the five barley loaves left over by those who had eaten. [14] After the people saw the sign Jesus performed, they began to say, "Surely this is the Prophet who is to come into the world." [15] Jesus, knowing that they intended to come and make him king by force, withdrew again to a mountain by himself.

... [25] When they found him on the other side of the lake, they asked him, "Rabbi, when did you get here?" [26] Jesus answered, "Very truly I tell you, you are looking for me, not because you saw the signs I performed but because you ate the loaves and had your fill. [27] Do not work for food that spoils, but for food that endures to eternal life, which the Son of Man will give you. For on him God the Father has placed his seal of approval."

... [35] Then Jesus declared, "I am the bread of life. Whoever comes to me will never go hungry, and whoever believes in me will never be thirsty."

Little me
BIG GOD

Collect the series

- The Man Who Would Not Be Quiet • Never Too Little • The Best Thing To Do
- The Dad Who Never Gave Up • The Boy Who Shared His Sandwich
- The Easter Fix • The Little Man Whose Heart Grew Big
- How Can I Pray? • The House That Went Splat • The Christmas Surprise

The Boy Who Shared His Sandwich
© Stephanie Williams, 2021. Reprinted in 2021, 2022, 2023, 2024.

Published by:
The Good Book Company

thegoodbook.com | thegoodbook.co.uk
thegoodbook.com.au | thegoodbook.co.nz | thegoodbook.co.in

Unless indicated, all Scripture references are taken from the Holy Bible, New International Version. Copyright © 2011 Biblica. Used by permission.

Stephanie Williams has asserted her right under the Copyright, Designs and Patents Act 1988 to be identified as the author and illustrator of this work.

All rights reserved. Except as may be permitted by the Copyright Act, no part of this publication may be reproduced in any form or by any means without prior permission from the publisher.

ISBN: 9781784985837 | JOB-007879 | Printed in India